Never Née Fey

poems by

Dana Miller

Finishing Line Press
Georgetown, Kentucky

Never Née Fey

Copyright © 2023 by Dana Miller
ISBN 979-8-88838-368-1 First Edition
All rights reserved under International and Pan-American Copyright Conventions. No part of this book may be reproduced in any manner whatsoever without written permission from the publisher, except in the case of brief quotations embodied in critical articles and reviews.

ACKNOWLEDGMENTS

Publisher: Leah Huete de Maines
Editor: Christen Kincaid
Cover Art: Dana Miller
Author Photo: Jana Brandelik
Cover Design: Hot Rod Walt and Sharlene Richards

Order online: www.finishinglinepress.com
                  also available on amazon.com

Author inquiries and mail orders:
Finishing Line Press
P. O. Box 1626
Georgetown, Kentucky 40324
U. S. A.

Table of Contents

Part 1: Viologens

Multum in Parvo	1
Oyster Card	2
Princely Pornography	3
Cumberland Rum Nicky	4
Manannán mac Lir	5
Tattered Empress	6
The New Favorite	7
In the Lo-Fi Whorehouse with the Neon Carpet	9
Dybbuk of my Daymares	10
Recrucify, Then Rewind	12
Last Halloween in Hawaii	13
Random Bedlam	14
Appaloosa Legs	15
The Louder Wish	16
Virgin Cashmere	17
Waif of the Weft	18
Wild Swimming	19
Zelotypia	20
Pit Viper Cypher	21
Marmaduchess	22
Années Folles	23
Dicentra Spectabilis	24
Gannets	25
High July	26
It Glows Under the Half-Smirk	27
Last Lighthouses	28
MX-76	31
My Time and Other Gate-Kept Institutions	32
Ogham and Béaloideas, My Mouth Education	33
Printed With Ibex	34
Spent Force	35
Double Termination Points	36
Letterato	37
Not a Facsimile of Rain	38

Eyes Like the Gmork 39
Like Hartshorn and My Lipizzan Powers 40
Isn't He Killing? 41
Wavelet Well Met 42
Sauterelle 43

Part II: Concrete Vellum

(G)lover 47
A Saturnian Day 48
Bottlecap Butterfly 49
Colloidal Glass Transition 50
Memory of a Memory 51
Mint Metallic 53
Opallios 54
Season of the Neverwas Boy 56
Plongée 57
Soft Costs 58
Constituent Colors: Ode to a Locust-Born Butterfly 59
Sprunny 61
The Pegasus Sanctions 62
Open Fetch 64
Best Legs in the Baptist Church 65
Chaperone Shoes 66
Hail Mary Pass 68
Wings of Wax on the Dais 69
June Plum 70
Atomic Heels 71
Cold Air Pictures 72
Moon Madlings 73

For all the storybook wingéd things, for all that natural-born glitter brings, for every last one of the forest's wildest and most wolfish greenlings, and especially.....*for The Vines.*

Part 1: Viologens

Multum in Parvo

I sat in a dress pooling like satin Cabernet;
I watched the dawn go down on the day—heard Cobras hissing final rhythmic threats,
my mirror a black and tarnished bet.
Carrying a buckeye in my right pocket
singing behind the plow.....

I pull my bobby socks up to my knees; these days I swarm like runaway bees.
100 miles of good road between, gun-hungry and godless—a tousled Didoleen.
Ode to the blades on my back....

They'll put you in one of their bins,
That's what they do when you're smarter than them.

Nobody remembers Sinatra for box sets and concept albums;
It was the press gang in the peach fog, big-wave butterflies and retrospect in rawdog.
A steady diet of left-handed cigarettes and Sami glow cake
makes for anticlockwise
bluebirds—and oh yes, those kinds of pablums.
Meanwhile, his scratch vocals sound like mystic topaz...

Doyenne of all your little hells,
I was running your Iditarod barefoot.
Drowning like dembow in the fountain outside your priory,
pouring luminol across every one of your lissome lies....
not as if it it was ever needed in order to see them from space.

My fireplace is cold now—and used only to store books

Oyster Card

There's nothing sweet about fanatics, you said,
Casbah under carpets and Topper nearly dead—everywhere but on the radio.
Blando, blando
Turn that rabble!
You sent me top of the pops;
You taught me to conquer the charts, duty-free.

Found all my riches in what I did not have,
learned new hours in the day.
Figured out how to make the limit the zillion stars,
dreamed I took Billy Redden to L.A.….

From then on I broke into my own rehearsals;
You told me if I was ugly, I was in.
A walking advert for toothless, pussy-whipping grins,
Your kind of handsome—the fatal sin.

And there's Strummer napping in a midday grave
And there's Lydon door-breaking—that classist stun grenade.

Didn't matter now the vultures—
Didn't amount to the tortures—

All of us leftover 101ers the minute you fade away,
forever your shoelace baby.

Warring brothers and Sandinistas still beat Sinatra,
for the invention of sick jokes and predictable pitfalls.
You do your wilderness penance and then you're just a hippy with zips,
black market voodoo still selling that gene memory.

Princely Pornography

Trilling like a selkie—mere constellation epitaph...
her, the curated coda of your grimoire.
My hands hoarse from the pantomime—a nickel and diming of the heart...

Do they make coronation logs for characters like yourself?
—abdicators of all that could ever be called true.

As you pour Cutty Sark from the coffee cup behind your back,
you sidle up to the next doormat,
love-doco in double lutz.

You don't have to be a Redgrave to post bond for the IRA.
I did it on a teacher's salary; I did it to dim the day.

mother of all sequencers—
bucolic.
I see your feet; I hear them frolic,
you think you win—aren't you so symbolic....

red jellyfish lightning—
alcoholic.
Your fetid megaphone; my Capulet colic,
lurid lies and defamations—my, how your doom pariah rollicks...

Our imaginary relationship is so much cooler than our real-time one—
Mrs. Huckleberry Finn and her two-string symphony.

A plectrum drawing blood...

There are always two deaths: the petaflop one and the one people see.
You're a low cowboy who has lost his crow;
Nothing but the hoax in the Wild West medicine show.

Cumberland Rum Nicky

Lord High Executioner and his opulent ornaments,
Something like postulant porn…...spirit trinkets,
Quartermaster from the IRA watched them back a pig into the crowd that day,
But it was you—you were the violent agent of change.

You brandish your theodolite everywhere you go,
But I was the only one to measure the angles of your heart's mange,
Sluicing like sweet williams—no lover's luck at all….
Living and dying in the transept of your sculpin church.
To the victor goes the spoils.

Manannán mac Lir

I didn't know if it could quite be,
because of their wind vane loyalty—
and because you've been to the moon and I to Hell.

For all those years I walked behind who I thought was king,
draped in moonlight fur.
Now they all kiss *my* ring.

It was that I knelt in my shrine to verse,
that's what the men of the Word will tell you is so perverse
about me.
I ran my heart out for them with all the fealty of horses
until I began to see.

But he
never tires of watching me nock and draw—
the tip of my arrow the only steeplejack in his skutch-yard.

Tattered Empress

You never understood the great cloud maraud,
that you had won every tournament.
Even tracing specters, you taught them what Black Maria meant
—riots in the orchard.

Love is everything, love is sacred, love is your last chance.
No. Love is just a friend to dressmakers.
Slightly more fun than the funeral.
The moment you enter the rath: the music of the shaken chain.

They like you worn on the collars and cuffs,
in a pleasing state of decay.
Her love was past its "sell by" date,
but every party needs performers.

Ever and still, you will find her a cocoon in cling
—a perpetual motion Colleen—
bedecked in the pastel emeralds of the rose renaissance.

The New Favorite

I don't say he wouldn't anymore
I've learned too late that 'sweet' will rot you to the core
It's a singing beach where
the nautilus and the night-time shopper
doing dark 80s rad
make free with the midnight lightning and the streaking Sarin gas.

You think you'll make me Basil Brown but you will soon learn, also too late
It's all just a Bactrian betrothal whether you wish it so or not, you derivative bore
and eavesdropping on elegance is all you've ever got, hmmmmm....still sore?
Good. To your everlasting chagrin,
you will find I have disappeared like Shergar long before you turn halfway round again.

You love like the Cailleach;
I love like intarsia.
But I hardly notice anymore.

Now, now! Isn't that just the candy way!

I came back home in winter and found myself waiting in the door—
between 1 & 2 on the East 4
still smell like dead rabbits, we gravediggers from Galway
Only now I am slow-gear driving through the fast-falling snow on the mountain road ......
........just between the twists in the lore
of here and true native.

Here, here! Let me clink you proper!
or kick in your teeth and call it kinetic art.

blissfully alone on a Saturday night and sincerely blasting Chumbawamba.....
just before......
I punish you in your own medium, all the way this time,
once and for all.
No manzanitas, no monkey flowers.
I will make you pay in the same currency that you sold me for
—only more, so very much more.
And I will do every bit of this even as I, biscuit and ball,
return to my cherished Alphabet City,
watching all

my eternal connection to this place skitter along the sidewalks under ChinaTown lanterns and away across Canal.

Never again to be your dacha, never again even your Dana!
Finally free of your emotional gore,
Never to breathe your damage,
Never to feed your poor.

All hail the cladding on this sun-built emporium of vain-gorgeousness!

Take both knees now if you are wise;
the new favorite is on the rise.

In the Lo-Fi Whorehouse with the Neon Carpet

You hang on to the wish;
you've lost all your deference.
Claw ground down to ash,
blunted by the extraordinary lies you tell when you're poor.
You left me on the lithophane but you made a crucial mistake:

—-you thought I would stay—-

Brimstone butterflies don't sit for your sick songs
and I'm no longer your palace slave.
I was the invisible ondist in the country of your nectar-venom;
just wait til it's Juno Temple or Zoe Kazan playing me in the movie
—that'll show em.

Push me out, jumpmaster,
you know it don't sing.
You and your capital chemicals
got you more than all the love I could bring.

—like Bret was L.A. but New York was all Jay—

contraceptive cocaine sold on a matchstick galleon,
legs like rainbow eucalyptus tree,

I suppose it could have been you,
We both know it wouldn't be me.

Dybbuk of my Daymares

I never had a taste for your tiny dreams,
never could get my mouth around your casuist cut creams
It was always my body and your snatch.
You're just another common rule follower;
perhaps that's why you were so shocked that I didn't follow any of yours?
Perhaps that's why you were just the knob
and I am still The Doors.

The fact that I take in the moment greater than you makes me your mother superior,
not the whipping post for your gnarled self-blame.
You: absurdly lobbying for bicycles on highways when you're the murder semi
on every lane.
Try every Twit-ffirmative Action sop in your shriveled sack, baby.
You will only ever be a twat twiddling his thumbs.

My body harbored your acts of rescue like it did your throwaway twins,
like Red Riding Hood's basket for hire,
and maybe a week beyond that—just to draw your ire.
The 'twirlers,' you called them, and I thought:
One for each hand, like drumsticks. This must be the beat.

Spin your sticks as you might,
you couldn't make a fire in our or any other home;
your other helmet ever pointing toward your Rome.
Nothing is ever warm but the fury you feed on when
you can't shred me like you did all the documents that held the ugly truth.
You can't shred, period. It is something only rockstars do.

When you "asked" me to put them through your megalomaniacal meat grinder too,
I did that because I loved you
—but really only up to that day.
No, I didn't want them either, but not that way.
I think now how glad I am they retracted their periscopes, free will or no.
They were your betters too, in their bled-red peacoats.

What did it matter, all in all?
Anything you made is going to have that kind of pall,
and you made a pollinator's paradise of every girl,
then disappeared

at the first sign of real Rumspring-ahhh (pleading the rum, but falsely).
I am content to seek the cool pocket in the sheets
with my inquisitive toe, with my unburned wing.

Recrucify, Then Rewind

Drinking electric venom under madder-hydrangea,
dreams and thighs, pure vanilla-strawberry slack.
You wouldn't know that we call it "pink" all because of jagged dianthus;
you aren't a gardener, don't know how to grow anything,
but you're going to need this time on your back.

For all your black and white world,
the unslakeable color saturation (to the point of pigment thrombosis)
tracks you like a falcon.
And, like the pilot's leg you inherited,
it lies brumating for you in the quickened intramural warfare of your Dorian-soon attic.
The pace is hot.

It's still me.
Maslow's bitchocracy, in kinetic type no less.
The rare combination of high wind and bright sunlight.
Wind-chime cadences you have no rhythm for.

I never dressed for you; I dress *at* you.
I get a snarky laugh out of the way your paper-doll proportions
don't suit my Chrome Hearts leather bikini.

I used to feel such pity for you; it was the nation of my first emotion at the sight of your face.
This was the fisherman-woven willow that cauterized us together,
but you didn't figure that out
until the very end (neither did I).
Much the same as the way I felt for the broken fox's jaw I found lying out destitute,
sunbleached, and dirty by the propane tank one day long after your skeletons ran
their tuneless bones far from my closet.
You were equally overpowered and overshadowed by the modernity huddling next to you
in the form of my timeless adoration, I reasoned.

I left that bone out there, as I left you, to remind me of what ephyra can do.
At night I do sometimes worry that it gets cold,
but this doesn't mean I will ever again love you.
Everyone forgets that type was born moving, not static,
and mine will be your gut-braiding Gravitron long past your grave.

Last Halloween in Hawaii

A wave breaks in a place that is half as deep as the wave is tall.
If the rail is too low, you claw into the curl;
if it's too high you become the world's least rad rhino-chaser—straight into the soup.

The ultimate middle finger is to leave with your name,
carve it with an ice pick,
jagged as Jagger, across the back of Jeff Beck's guitar like Tina Turner did—
because Jeff is cool enough to love that the way any honest man should.
Meanwhile, the sleaze who tried to invent you with said name,
on a continent you gave him no less,
is still running the same tired, back-alley barf-game. (Yeah, okay barno!)

He'll only ever be remembered
as the Bucks Fizz version of "What's Love Got To Do With It."
The gross kind of hot-dogger. Never a wave-slider.
One who had to pull leashes to win.
And these are the comments of his friends.

Over here, I am shimmying down the stages he didn't have the crest to ever set foot on.
We always knew I had the sand, didn't we?

Telling them to keep the current under me,
I keep the pulse in my pocket.
I'm just about ready to get more than compliments for all of this,
about to cash in on every single thing you missed.

I've studied hard and I've learned
even the tame impalas have to run fast to catch their connections.
Kevin Parker said:
"there are definitely things that have disappeared that would have been great."
The greatest of all is that I know you are not one of them.
The second is that wavelengths like him made me know it wasn't too late.

Random Bedlam

The panorama of nevers
never ceases to amaze;
the turning of the worm
formats the turning of the screw.
The tiny mayhem, the considerable heaven.

When the rest of me goes to obsidian
in the octopus-ink dark, you can't tell the difference.
Can't see the sun in eclipse season.

All of our old favorite vandals and scandals
—-dendritic starfish on a calico cloud.
Teaching you the traces was a patchwork terror,
but, all full-margin ruptures included,
I still very much like what you're like.

Appaloosa Legs

You made art constellations out of my sand flea bites;

I made a cross-country lipstick run in a Cady dress.

You never sell me the cheap trips;

you confiscate my sorry floods with your electrogram lips.

The Louder Wish

Eating cookies at the bar,
I found ceiling tones the rubato way.
Hooked on ups like the first waaaaave…..rockers in those supersensualist days.

Summoning your kisses with conditions,
your bones all piezoelectric.
Cloud native, rails of blow,
Super wolf moon and miles to go.

Nightjars, mauve and rhubarb…..
You're mad at me because you can't choose
when you full well know it's all I ever knew how to do.
You say my winning way is cheating,
you call his winning days defeating,

I say not everything best is fleeting…...

Virgin Cashmere

You will be crashing like king tides—-
when the scapegoat becomes the martyr.
Walking the songlines of your elders—torrefied.

I sew your postcards into my hem.
Pain made me ready,
anger made me pure.
I traveled alone to the secret sky—where tree sap turns into jewels.

Footfast—like my farthest-flung wish,
he came…
A badly behaved rabbit—Arcanum of fame.

I put on lip gloss and think of flowers—this keeps me '90s skinny,
in my potluck corduroys and the snow you made swirl in my room.

Waif of the Weft
    (an ode to Margot Fonteyn)

Everyone should become an invention like you insisted.
Change their noses, change their names, keep them all twisted—like your ankles.
Never your endless neck line.

Two forced extractions later, not one of them could match the inconstancy of your constant.
You brought your country fans even after the war.
They were down on their knees when you came to New York.

But love makes you capable.
No pauper's grave could ever hold you—only Nureyev.

Wild Swimming

On a day a daisy squinted in the sun,
I was being tolerated because of how much I loved and not because I was loved back.
Taking all my headliner color cues from a bleached Coke can I passed on my run.
Martello tower, you, and the torments of Gehenna—hour by hour.

He came out of the white noise, prophet of the tropics;
there was blood dried on the walls from a life fading three years before...

Love is the abortion you give your brain;
if it takes, you're the velvet revolution atop his refrain.
No one sees me home alone on a Saturday night,
drinking Matcha tea and eating cherry blossom stingers,
wishing I was Larkin Poe and catching up on Harmony Korine films I missed
because I was too busy wasting my non-refundable time loving your monster movie.

Dancing with my Moss legs in the cottage you'll never see,
loving every mistake in the boundless me you'll never be,
going back to my original birthright kind of free,
Blissfully—Like I never knew you....

Zelotypia

a vast catalog of sound
a world of boys that never would let me down
everyone looks prettier at Christmas

people think it moves like water but for me it runs like sand
—a little bit blows away from the top
and then surges back again
it's revenge to a girl but jealousy to a boy.

buy a dress—it hides the mess—it folds the press and runs.....like hose
they only circle when you struggle—when you're fit you've lost the bit
they will never see you dance around your bedroom so happy to be alone
—so honest on your own
too blind to admire the wind braids in your multicolored merfairy mane

I'm a half-breed dog but a very rare metal
a whim of iron who freely loots the dead
kisses like sour mash whiskey
I made 'late to the game' look new in history
damndest deadstick landing in all the heartland alley.

Pit Viper Cypher

Thousands of light-years—not so fast—as the escape velocity of my tears.
Remember: pulsars are embers of dead stars.

The Monk, the It Boy, and I, we're set to re-conquer the world together.
Why don't you build something holy out of your Antioch heartwood?

Your washed-up kind of feckless fell out of fashion some while ago, as in: on the first day.
The way your shoddy band thinks that not being able to really play or sing
is your calling card,
but in actuality it's just breathing proof of the fact you were never the artist in the room.
That was *always* me.

I was the thoroughbred;
and that was the one and only way or time you were ever my groom.

Marmaduchess

I could smell fame and greatness coming since I was the smallest child.
I was never built for your tiny version of events.
I smelled the potions in the dew,
The spell-telling roses twining round the Terebinth, teashur, and tamarisk trees….
These were gifts for which I should never have had to apologize to you.

All the verve the vivacaine had lent—couldn't half match me.
And yet here I am, holding all your hours...
And here I am, Ophelia fresh out of flowers….

Be a star wherever they will let you.

Années Folles
    (Mad Years)

Our flying colors and our blooming days,
I could never trade,
not for all the animal crossings in Arcadia.

Mom saying the teddy bear "made music"
and how I then spent the morning washing its feet,
being all but their Nine Days Queen—the wild brigantine.

Sea-drawn rocks sink differently.

Dicentra Spectabilis

City of love by way of Oz,
like the mimosas, we were only there to serve the flowers.
Testing the edges of a word, sprawled across the glass-topped dance floor, all hours.

Panther prowling beneath our feet like Limelight,
Pluvian Jupiter like Saturday morning sleep—
but if a beautiful title is only half the battle…....you'll be famous entirely.

Gannets

Once in a miracle moon,
the dawn will draw a bead on the day
for the white ravens who are punk-rock loitering on your destiny's flipgrid
—chancy as plutonium,
smelling of quince and calamondin,
looking through lupine freckles,
licking leaf-laden wolf eggs, speckled.

You'll go out to water your favorite maidenhair fern,
(it's doing so well on the porch this year)
and you'll discover in its pot the perfect, newly expired body of a naked hatchling bird,
not a day out of the oology unit and still a mile from weighing an ounce.
A cutting of a different sort.

Because you can't bring yourself to bury the Thumbelinian thing just yet,
you'll sit out on the swing next to it,
uselessly hoping to see a Lilliputian upheaval in its breast,
writing your next acrylic aegis
wearing nothing but your three-days underwear,
in the same flat mask of sunshine
that is filled by the Pemberlyn orange of its mother's distressed calls.
They lay like discarded rinds amidst the Campanula.

Hours later, you'll catch another glimpse of it as you come in from one of your night runs
down the old dirt road
—the teeniest chase van ever—
its downy would-have-been feathers in a dead heat with the color of the waxing dusk,
to a tone.

You do your post-leg-thrash stretch-out with its closed eye in your peripheral vision
—a bird bismillah.
At last the freshly dug bursary that will play home to your latest Angel Trumpet acquisition
(symbolically bought at the annual plant sale of the city's oldest cemetery)
will serve as its regenerative under-tomb as well.
That one has been overdue for planting by weeks and is sure to value the company.

Some afternoons curl like fawns in the glen;
others are a dogfight all the way to the wire.

High July

A sunset walk in the high blue,
one of those days that stretches so far you can't believe the morning belongs to the afternoon,
or that either could ever become a night.

I would have been here sooner
but I was busy cleaning up the mess that came from trying it your way,
shoving past the bootblacks and venerable metallurgists.

1000 years of dreaming at your feet and this is all it got me—behind.

I wrote our Midsummer vows on a ream accidentally smeared with bug blood.
You know how it is with cosh boys…..

But Carter was elected with those rock-n-roll funds
and you know Twiggs Lyndon—he ain't the only one.

Blues invocations in southern graveyards seem to stick—like faulty ripcords.

It Glows Under The Half-Smirk

the things you learn while killing yourself…
down the end of your own dick,
I got my comeuppance quick.
this wasn't like ingestion of the ancestor.

the things you'll hear in a drowned meadow…
I used to think you were a nice bunch of guys,
ever out of cigarettes, packs on packs of lies.
You thought you burned all the blooms of my life.
Shark-faced cars for the shark-toothed wife

the way things will phrase themselves in a dream…
the porcelain horseshoes of your bent vision.
the drugs in your dance have all ditched me, by and by.
what's left is streaks of lightning-blonde—celestial harlot dye.

no truck now for the very idea of you,
the two times needles,
the twice j'taime.
whyever wouldn't I get off my face?
it's hard, after all, to have fins in this place,
where pelicans regard the curvature of the world,
and your doormat-ador jeers through spikenard in gorged stantias—
seven full galaxies of *dream on.*

Last Lighthouses
(a riff for the faithless majority)

You'll come to know the type
You've given them all 13 years or more—full of hummable introspection
and the most famous rock stars in the world—to say nothing of your dose-dense soul
bandying about your hopes and fears
built entirely on bracellae and boustrophedon
They will come to your birthday parties and you will go to them at Christmas
It will seem the safest and most naturally warm thing in the world to lean your full weight on the concrete of their love
(though you might as well be giving birth in the High Arctic)
Ta, but how the best ones will swear they love you
Til you roundly disappoint yourself and believe
It's only when your weight-bearing hand goes crashing through what you thought was such an indomitable, vertical construction of care that you see it was always made of wet newspaper—and *you*, my dear, are just a penny gaff girl in the back rooms of their subconscious public houses
Then, they'll quietly sneak round the sticky corners of your rawest self
—of the actual show-up time—like white privilege guilt-trippers always do in the face of the real ghetto
into invisibility
into convenience
into convention
into covering for him—he is their son, after all
(even if they would say they didn't raise him to act like this)
there are twins here for sure, but never once (or ever) a twin flame.

To the comforts of conformity, even your last lighthouses will bend
Away from responsibility and respectability
Away from decency
and all their debts you owe
Away from everything you thought they'd be
weddings don't count, didn't you know?
Ohhh........You thought they meant always?
worse: you thought they meant like *you* do—didn't you?
Oh what a laugh-a-minute you are
Remember?
They even told you how funny and fun you are for parties they don't admit going to
What a lift you give to others, they praise!
What a joy to all their days!
you should always be around, except when you shouldn't.
and *you*, precious little idiot, you believed there weren't any shouldn'ts

just because you don't have any for them—didn't you?
Awww....did you write them a Valentine too? Ha.
Sorry, but the joke's absolutely on you.

When you've been dead about a week
curled up like a conch
on the kitchen floor
sobbing hysterically, on the hour every hour, like a beaten child and every bit as confused
watching the door and mapping the bruise
This is when you'll realize that they have always been irrelevant
It was only ever *your* heart feasting on the time
their mouse
your elephant
—trunk and memory, that is.
For a flash your tear-gasps will morph into insano-giggles
as you imagine telling them to go fuck themselves straight off
Then you dream of tricking them into a lunch date
where really you're going to FedEx their whole human bodies,
post haste,
to the same ruinous wasteland where they've so nonchalantly annexed you
But you can't find the address. Even after sifting meticulously through whatever shards
remain of your blown-out heart, it isn't there. Damn.
Lucifer probably bought it off Judas and stuffed the only copy in his back pocket
for safekeeping.
In Hell all the prettiest ones are sooo smart,
like they always said *you* were
Funny.

Rolling over to try and die one more time again,
you will bump noses with the one and only Michael Hutchence,
right there stretched out next to you, but not quite how you always dreamed it
rather like a canebrake of the afterlife
like an invigilator
this is autoplatonic strangulation after all
Devil Inside and that
Oh God, how you love(d) that bacchus boy
Oh Mab, how you willed this fall
Eventually, once you've died all you can die and died some more
something invisible will remind you of Patti Smith
and you'll remember that you have to get up
off the kitchen floor
You still have to stand up every day and dress in battered menswear like her so you can write
revolutionary poems—but be the kind of skinny only artistic girls can get

Even if you don't yet
have a Robert Mapplethorpe to switch stripey shirts with
in the paint-spatter of afternoon light
Even if you still relentlessly wait for them sometimes
late, later, latest in the grin-less night.

MX- 76

Sneerwise, I've seen better
Dearborn, without the metal
I'd go on to abort you like any other paperweight hitchhiking across my belly
and just that fast
Gutted? Hardly.
For who could ever trust their gut again til the gangrene of you was cut from it?
Anything to be shot of your sentences.
Grace Kelly has figured out the new math,
I'm afraid
and lordess, but you're a strict equation
Despite the munitions manifest
under the crown of your abdication
I just keep on loving you like caloric restriction and late-70s cocaine
stretching myself out like St. Swithin's Day across your salt lick
whole oceans of Tawny Kitaen
Ready
for my Helen Reddy moment
I'd sober up if I were you
The flecks of Roberta Flack in me will leash every lime tiger
leaping out of your 43rd-floor window with a piano strapped to its back.

My Time and Other Gate-Kept Institutions

Despite what you may have heard
I am no one's David Kammerer.
Though surely that wasn't from lack of effort on behalf of the "experts" in honor slayings.
I realized far too late in life how many doors Lucien Carr has left out of in my life.

However, there were two West Ends,
everyone forgets.
Interestingly, Carr rides and pseudocides are still free and fake in both,
but mine is the seed sovereignty you've never seen yet.

I am now completely fluent in the black cuneiform of the born rent boy.
It's alright though, Allen baby.
They only have to leave because they know before you do they'll never live up to your words.
You tell them about their form and meter when they can't tell themselves.

Put a silencer on the slaughter in the stockade, would you?
Go back to the beginning.
Stay smutty and absurd.
You're the sugar cube baby; you have my unbendable word.

But keep your dedications to yourself
because the sublime sortilege of delicious solitude is forever
the only signpost of the real saboteur.

Ogham and Béaloideas, My Mouth Education

I tend toward an open warp in honeyed parables.
I didn't see the rainbow bending but it sure saw me;
it was the year I started living as the artist I have always been, you see.

It was the year I was to conjure Bloomsbury in its fullest,
the way I once did every effortless
breath I took at Oxford,
that last summer before *him*.

It is still so much more than passion and posters.

Printed With Ibex

I don't even mind that you reheat your tea;
there's a whole Tiking tribunal that has no idea what Turtle Wax smells like.
Meanwhile, you. In your male cronedom, sipping social morsels on old sin frontiers,
divine and depraved, spiked like the highway trash made the sole province of the taken.

These somnambulists and sparrowhawks,
they want you to lease their filter-feeding affections for the day
—lactic and lazy—
like teen tearaways.
Completely unaware (as they picket and pine for today's "nonconformist" natural law)
of just how unrenovated they are in their own implicit lockstep.
More front than Harrods.

Italian plonk is precautionary medicine to many, I'm told.
Not as demotic as detonation trading in mythology—never half so bold.

Then me, with my radiused fretboard, wending to the will of the wood.
I'd rather drink the runnels of pastel sherbet off my own chin,
taking the Turing bite in rock pools like Anaglypta wallpaper.
Small-batch vinegar flying the banner of laminar flow—
—*lip logo* of a shrew.
An ocean archivist sidestepping your elephant cull.

I care not a fig for your transatlantic slander.
All argots are eventually dispossessed.
I've always been in the biological business of permanence alone
and you can watch as my vermillion burst outlasts your every accelerando.

Girls like me are meteorological conditions and harlequin geometry.
Pristine comets, pajama sharks.
The syrup in the sermon is my own eponymous thunder.
Rest assured, your ears couldn't earn it given ten lifetimes of nothing but explicit instructions.
Take your animal panic and your hippie heroes too.
Take your assegai and your holographic tracksuits.
I'll keep the omnichord in my wave garden any day and every way,
getting fiber-optic goosebumps in places unknown to you
—or any of your kind.

Spent Force

I galloped like Jesus across your quicksand values.
You sent me a love note a day for years.
Then, the moment the hydra beast re-sketched me for you,
you heard just what a deaf eye hears.

One was my protégée...
One was my clone...
The first took my stage name, the second my phone.

The A with the French filched my stance.
The A with the shorts pilfered my pants—only to gloat.

Teeming with the confidence that transcends bad memories,
your dollar-store Yorke voice...
all lysergic avarice for that cherry Rolls Royce.

I got a Bible from each grandmother, one great and one small.
I prayed to the sacrosanct smell of a Walmart greeter's vest,
like a ladybug assassin,
 ruthless as a rapier to this very moment.

Double Termination Points

It was only the high-heat blushes,
the blazing tundra under my skin,
that ever burnished you so bright
—-turned you into the daydreamer with the dangling leg—
Plus Reagan.

To that point, I should have fallen in love with my own reflection that night.
Narcissus and Boldfrond.
These rural American boys have a vicious time coming to terms with what they are not.
Anything true you say about other places (read: other men) is commie Europhagia.

They are used to slapping one another's backs and running around the playpen
of their made-up masculinity together,
throwing tantrums like toddlers
but always making sure to insist what real men
they are!
Sam Elliott's mustache.
This is their only "always."
What a gas.
I love nothing so much in the world as when the joke's on the ones too busy actively
being the joke to know.

There's this teeth-to-toe dance they do with their also-ran status,
and when they feel it teeter (like their daunting bellies), this is your fault too
because you had enough worldly experience to factually explain it.
That's to say nothing of having the vocabulary too!
Suddenly they're the City Amish and you're the skirt steak.
You should be smart enough to know that's not what such a 'big mouth' is for.
hot damn at the (W)horripilation
you bring.

It's forever fascinating to see who someone becomes when they have the blind upper hand…

Letterato

Full snow moon is done tilling;
don't forget: just one romaction per shilling.

We talk click-dirty to one another like coconut crabs.
He likes his truth cheated quite a bit to the left.

I stand like a Ronette Tim Burton might have made.

First three Jupiter moons, all alchemical acts;
take the bet: the redemption engine,
like all the best harlots and hacks.

All the never-saids beaten to a Lambeg drum,
every animal interrelation in the root cellar,
turtle and caterpillar.
You and the Derry big slapper.

Heads of decapitated porcelain
lying in sideways stares
like dynastic boxwood hedges cut aslant.

I spelled out his letters in ballast;
I tell you, I loved the bloke...
and all this I carried on the back you broke.

Not a Facsimile of Rain

The crippled piano player slides twisted arms into metal crutches
with all the delicate prowess of a dark duchess,
with all the eccentricity of Diana Vreeland.
He can still play the songs but he can't sing them.

Drinking from a fur teacup
—with the palinode moon upon a stick.

What must it be like to be too significant for words?
What would it feel like to walk in excuses like yours?
People like you don't even realize that spiderwebs make a sound.

Eyes Like the Gmork

surveillance stare
he smells like rained-on ferns if they were made of mackerel clouds
he dreams in colors only hummingbirds see
i wear my white armband oh-so-sincerely…..

lips edge-curling like fleur de lise
mother of pearl, le fairy piece.

Like Hartshorn and My Lipizzan Powers

There was still so much to uncover back then
when I was a sprat in a dissenting chapel
carrying my kiss of charity with total impartiality
in a backpack spilling with all my other spirit flames I didn't yet guess were offal.
There were angels in the trees of Peckham Rye in those days,
and their sororal needlewomen were like choristers dressed in Sinead shorts,
with spiderwings.

This all happened in a place of mirror-lowlands and mechanical meteors,
on an obverse Isle of Dogs
—scattered with sectaries that were to sunder me straight.
The first time I ever disrobed you (with my teeth, let's not miss)
Balliol's marks glowed back at me from all the places on your skin
I had thought to kiss.
Stripping my starry mantle, you encountered another breed of brand altogether.
I have it on good authority that you're never to recover.
Witchfinder General that you were,
you still found my aerial devices of sedition as infuriatingly elusive as
William Blake's grave—and maybe that hotly contested too.
There was a subversive futurity to the way you grew to be grampus.
For all my numinous furore
and despite the fact that convulsionists before me as Camorra-famous as Shelley
had sent whole Declarations of Rights across the moors in miniature hot air balloons
way ahead of my tigerseed perigee,
I was to be a relegated relict
and you were to cave completely to your Procrustean race memory.
There was nothing for it.
Ack, well.
At least I was the most stylized riot in all the land,
and there will always be liriope and lemon button fern, for cheer.

You might almost be commended for believing (so fervently, lest we forget)
That you really could drain the fens to banish my aquatic spirit's kin
and ever get these hundred Edens wet.
Whipping my Mick the Miller mind, you tripped the wire on quite a banshee bet.
There, within a certain sea to sky corridor,
I had and still have my own Girlingites' gospel
—and the heart of a boy who has spent his life catching comets in a butterfly net.
Word on the street is: it torments you yet.

Isn't He Killing?

black night glitter
strewn across his bedroom and the sea
walking the midnight streets never fails to overrate me

brunet stars sundered
it's a gentle brutality he delivers for free
in his Bon Jovi voice he serenades me

ripped up Beach Boy jeans and James Dean faded white tee

a lostling
a changeling
my darling Apollo

better watch your boy-cherry
you can't always look back and hate your youth
you'll grow down to be an adult if you're not careful
talking sententious chattel
deeply uncouth

Wavelet Well Met

Love makes a ceremony of everything.
Disguised as a boy, I fled your harem.
Quickly found myself robed in the troubles of a king;

Osiris knew less of dismemberment.
Performing my own caesareans,
reversing Tabitha's song.

Then
my words
like diving birds
reveled each night until dawn.

Sauterelle

Chapter 1: Selva Oscura (the first 10 paces of a divorce)

Like a cold-stunned turtle, both revived and brutalized by a rectal thermometer, Cymbie woke up on the incandescent beach of something like Half Moon Cay with the foam at her toes and the blood of her childhood pony encrusted on her pearline hands. Hands— she groggily thought. Empty containers people attached way too much meaning to. These particular chapped items of her own had played John Lennon's white piano. They had affixed the uninspired band stickers of her first boyfriend's half-defunct attempts at music to her naked, teenage body as an anniversary surprise and then peeled them off in the shower herself the next morning, with flailing anger and defeated bits of skin, after he failed to come home yet again that night. Hands did things like meet presidents and birth babies. They soothed circus lions and allowed blind people to "see." They collected and organized things of every nature. Things like shells. Girls like her. They recorded and erased whole histories. But…

Of any era there must be an end if it is to be defined. As with any death, the last few days of my marriage did nothing to prepare me for its automatic and permanent demise. I loved my husband. I love him still. But to successfully leave him I must focus on his weak points and not the lovely, glimmering shadow of what was once a great, though one-sided, love. I must drink the noxious nightshade potion (true vision) that would reverse the spell. I don't think they make antidotes for the kind of venom someone who is no longer complicit in your fairytale of them—because it is no longer serving their own selfish interests—can loose on a heart that knew no better. The pain is intense and fructified. Every moment it reinvents itself as a new specter of a former smile. I remember the shiny mornings of chemical poetry—I wonder if the drugs didn't do it—would we still part company? Will I ever indulge my hope again? For it feels like all feeling is hereby drowned. And with the same brash cruelty of a kitten in a bag. All the sweet moments of you and my family. Every flower, all the moons, a million parts to asymmetry. Our long history of pain and renewal stopped when I began. I remember I saw you, pitied you last. And I remember foreign sand.

The rapidity of my family's sloughing off of my marital facades both frightened and edified me. I am the most hateful of bitches. I saw his tatty suitcase half-packed and was glad it was leaving. But when he kicked it in regretful giving up/admittance one night when he was leaving, I cried for hours and knew it would be an image to haunt me for all time— also that these would be the last tears of my truest girlhood heart. The rest of me would cry differently from there forward. I saw his toolbox sitting dusty on a slanted shelf and sobbed in the remorse he would never feel.

Great philosophers say that such bathyspheres of coruscating pain are the only avenue to true growth and original sight—of character. I have lost my credible compass—and I do not trust a single chamber of my heart anymore. I was conscious on the day he left that it was my last silence. That the progression of clouds and clocks around me were in the last quarter of shielding me from what I had to tell. In just a few more ticks and flutters, I'd have to call them all and meet them all and form it. How strange that people think of leaving and separation as emptiness—truly its solid figure is more ominous and imposing than any tangible fear on earth. It hovers around your skin like an inverted-rapist you wish would sink in and attack but will only touch lightly at your sorest spots. I'd love to be a dame about all this. To light cigarettes and salute mornings with flipped hair in ornate bathrobes and long skinny jeans. To lope like a bored lagoon into the dynamo gustatory institutions of New York and order "diet ice" with a straight face. But I am a tiny girl.

And yet……..

My tiny life ended on February 6, 2005 and I didn't want to forget this married self, my only self, in lieu of a future, a freedom, or another married self. What was my lexis of cool again? Paragons of endless glamour, glamazons of mind and manner. I needed to decorate his departure with striations of Shinto sensibility. To remember that there are spirits in all things—even in divorces from men one never should have given a second glance toward.

Throughout the cavernous ruins of my life the smell of intrepid innocence has permeated—all the way down to the celestine clouds of Lethe—and back up again, to the big-tent hypergravity of a woman I knew it had always been my destiny to be. To the realization that *I* was the artist in the room. It had always been *me*—all that time I was hero-worshipping him. I was the enchanted coral *en ville*. I was, well and truly, the confetti cannon, the Milanese excess, and the jocular scrum. What time had I, then, for exoplanets?

Looking at his life-defunct face my first thought was: how odd for a champion narcissist to die with so few teeth. Funny that. This is what decimation and divorce sound like. Mega analog. Oh so very *handy*.

Part II: Concrete Vellum

(G)lover

bee stings and bared teeth,
running my switchblade tongue
right down your turned cheek.

the foot-rot of your fickle favor,
goblin candles lighting the cut under my eyebrow
tallow searing

some deal you daytime blows
others hand you dungeon keys
You take them the same way round your twisted bend
You bring them all faithlessly to their faithful knees

the things you were unaware of
could have filled all the concert halls you never will again.
You stay cozy in what you fear to acknowledge
just like people who look at denim and don't see sharecroppers and civil rights.

A Saturnian Day

There danced
oscillating gravity in the Neptune grass.
We had
a posy of swan's feathers on the second shortest day.
It was
not like Venus—she takes the long way—
(like the dispossession of my face).

Just remember:
if you don't agree with their definition of twilight,
they'll run through the streets with your head on a pike

We saw
the Luna moths on my Narnia lamp post.
I gave
private levitation sessions to the heaviest you of all.
I said
"you can be a caveman, but not a Neanderthal"—
(just help me make my mad maps before you beat the brawl).

Don't forget:
I keep my crows and my creatures fed
our cars hit the same deer on the same night and this is why we wed

I understood
how the vocoder warped the Aquarids.
You dodged
the midnight feast full of words you could never be friends with.

You lost:
George Sand meets Chopin
Juicy Fruit on Ferris Wheels—together, so strange
being creatively schizo—like Virgil Abloh and Isabella Blow

Elf owls,
they speak mythology without sentimentality.
They leave
one dreaming half to death—as ditch lilies growing off a Parisian garret might feel.

Bottlecap Butterfly

Chin lifted, shoulders back
I walked with a tiny sun balanced on my nose,
wanting everything to feel like the word "symposium" did on my untested tongue.

Things that smelled like my father's 1966 yearbook are of a Christloam fascination;
dirt is holy and fertile to the pagan.
I wore Rasta fishnets and Michaelmas daisies.
I was silver by nature
—a metacomet trailing her heartfelt hallucinations.

This was to be my silly season.
With a snowflake gravity, your collateral consequences descended
to dandruff my shoulders with your well-designed D-Team dementia.
Couture and death-still pharaohs could not have distracted me from it,
my hair snarling in smoke tangles,
my worst wish was a switchblade that folded in threes.

In my own cities of superlatives, they rode silver-maned dragons.
My ear that swiveled for ever-escalating Benders was full of the feeling of getting drunker,
and finding more and more boys that I thought were Judd Nelson
only caused my original girl-soul to send me an engraved invitation
back to the party I had forgotten I'd invented.

The second-rate bazaar of them all had not remotely revealed itself to me yet,
and I was top-to-tail Watership Downy Jr. as I contemplated the purity of rectangles
as well as what it might take from a boy for him to *really* become a master of foxhounds.
I was only ever after a trapeze tailpiece and a warm-leaning voice.

In this slippage of light, I never find you
and to this day I would rather tarry at the flea market where my grandfather worked,
bloodhounding the 25-cent, broken ceramic animals that no one else would think to buy
—for my curio that understood crystallography to mean something different.

Colloidal Glass Transition
(for Greg Gilbert)

I knew it would be today
because I knew you wouldn't let your last September
get away
—nor would it dream of leaving without you.

But you've left without me,
my mammalian transducer.

Female calves with twin brothers are often born infertile.
Many times they are taken for slaughter before they are even a few days old for this.
I frequently wonder: would I have been if the stars that made us knew about me and you
back when you were breathing.

What we were was written in the weald,
far out past where the women gather moss
and the naked cannabis children drive by, aflame.

In your after, every morning is a coin toss with mutated memories,
a fat quarter of Spoonflower fabric to never-patch the ever-rip of your body gone-ness.

Memory of a Memory

Riding along the bridlepath of my brother,
I was felled like an elm in your story.
There was dog rose, wood sorrel, and river flags;
we did the kind of lotus-eating that didn't occasion a song.

You telegraphed your stunt-moves just before you made them,
and I trained every day like Bruce Lee—to try to endure and defend you.
Your care came with cartridges like *The Odyssey*—I couldn't hook out the words.
But I knew you by smell identity
—inveigled victuals and gangplanks.
—bastard barbiturates and badger-toothed babies.

Ours was a love on a light table,
half-sips of heart in a physick garden,
malingerers and wands of hazel.
—the tabulating leather strop of you,
me, the teasel-blade dipped in poppy syrup.

There was a musical grammar to the way you screamed down the sky,
a rhythmic strum in how you decorated every lie—in one vestigial feature or another.
I would not decide on your Home Rule or any other, nor do I ever extend uneasy truces.
You made out our connection was the Curragh Incident but we both know better.

An acorn to the chest
Loping after the mining town sultans
As they always know best

The only place he was free was with his fists and his firsts.
With a head full of boiling lead, his were hasty, slipshod emotions;
Mine were parcels of poorly-sewn lace and other things of a star-like brightness,
the stitching on the shroud.

Under our wharf house lived a reticulate whipray.
His tiger-scapes were hum-colored
like the dampers of our glass piano.
There is a reason they are nicknamed "honeycomb stingrays."
All the while I was looking for the monstrous Ottoman poet,
a laudanum-licked boy to wear curlers and a fashionable clubfoot
—one who keeps foxes in drawing rooms overlooking ducks involuntarily ice-skating
on frozen ancestral ponds.

You were my tide-drink and I the silt in your shoe.
You tried your level best to elide over my parrot-like repetitions
as well as the holy hieroglyphics on my hand
—especially wherever yours naturally enclosed it.
I ran up holding honeycombs, the never-slumbering daughter of pink cheetahs.
Setting your gimlet gaze with planet-sized pupils, you could find an insult in a rosehip.
These outbursts of yours—all just the lame horses of your landlord.

They say the first woman was made from limbs of rowan,
and I am the woman who swallowed the moon,
reading the air like a falcon,
carrying my voice,
—stoppering the jar on yours.

We leave off, unconjugated,
largely because you do not know Latin
—or any other romance language—
only pigs and their frost-gilded squeals of sycophancy
—all those who merely wish to cut a lock of what was once your ruff
for their marmish mantels.

You still know "nowt" of allies or 'always'
and now likely never will.
You have shredded the marigolds that might have saved you,
scoring the ground where our possibilities passed through,
feverishly stricken with yourself, as if by the plague.

Your hands
that talked so emphatically across decades of my life have gone grave-silent,
your tongue the deafening defeatist that muted them
—and whatever might have been of *us*.

Mint Metallic

Sally the Swain was my breakdown voltage phaser,
all pommy standing there in the diarmuid wreaths.
Anything can take you to the teddybear hospital like that.
It could be oxeye daisies and tamarind treacle.
It could be neon fizz.
It could be a red fuzzy sweater and that twirling clock of the calque.

I crisscross the ocean with my leather steamer trunk
to our tumbledown cottage by the gemstone foam,
all stray capacitance and imaginary PB&J.
Nevermind you have beached sea dragons on purpose.

The same day I woke up in the paisley underground,
I dreamt you and I were the Disco Pigs
selling Pork Sitty, round and round,
naked eyes trained on Andromeda spiral.
Oh—you know my petal, forever chiral.

Like the golden blood of the aboriginal girl,
like the Junaluska apple found under the rat's last damn,
Night time 90s rockets, sunspheres, and Toad the Wet Sprockets;
This is what I am.

Opallios

The Isle of Dogs is no place for tumbling, demented poetry
and a mind that grows fables like Nile lilies.
I never knew the Northern Lights could be so localized, such fireless flames.
Believing there would be blue herons,
I blinked at the shoreline of your brazen famine far longer than any Bombette should.
There was only ever a halberd-holding stunt driver with a shark tongue,
and even he, at the last, said he wouldn't drive me home—even if he could.

There were purple provinces of mirror worlds, none benign.
There were pewter skies and ghost tides,
ever leading to stop-motion suicide.
Go, go, American goliath;
your heart will mean nothing but head-to-head buffalo to him,
and this you must taste early.

What had been my woodland symphony of steepled trees became an arbor of paper.
All my abature showed like dew-flecked metal fatigue across the meadow,
and I failed your old, gray whistle test for the first and final time right there.
There were to be no animal funerals in this Ophelia place.
I had blood like mercurial chaos and yet I spoke only Robin's egg blue,
suffocating in open air on the strange nomenclature and the tree-climbing serpent of you
—hung on the hotshot greed-gradients of your silver-soaked doom.

You slid on your side through goblin forests, undetected at first…
but for your slick, new skin—which caught the light at times in a way that announced
the malicious morse code that long ago relinquished your mind to the basilisk.
Introducing a higher order of hate,
you came breathing black stars at fathoms deep,
and ruthlessly pruning palisades of clouds into venomous vengeance machines.

I slunk upwind of your slaughterhouse,
still able to smell your furled lightning and the baffles on your gun,
pinned my ears to your power-words like 'lore' and 'dragon,'
trembling at just the wind-taste of your totemic ozone and Séverine sun.
I hurriedly and haphazardly hid my teal jungle under a rock-crystal chandelier,
aglow like the witching side of a polar ocean.

Fleeing the dungeon-dark of your Easter-killing tea parties,
the wild tattoo of fear animated my spearpoint dance and your mute moon studies.
As fate and girl-ruining stories would have it,

my fin-foot slipped on your arching arpeggio of swords like snow jazz,
and I fell
somewhere out towards Mars
right down through that hidden trapdoor that is chance
never stopping even to give my mother a signaling glance.

Sometimes in the winter, you'll have a bit of flaked, dead skin on a cumbersome part of your lip that requires a delicate mix of focused artistry and surgical precision to pull off without making your entire mouth bleed like a stuck pig. You can usually tell how close your fingernails are to the threshold of that little jigsaw piece of livid skin by the stinging pull that threatens to unshut fully if you tug, even gently or absentmindedly, in that dermal direction just once more. It is one of life's more dreadful shames that there is no equivalent hazard-portent for the people in your life for whom you must absolutely do the same—far more frequently, and with great, whole tablecloths of blood be damned.

Season of the Neverwas Boy

It took:

Fingers and toes of shock punk-pink,

coffee-flavored ice cream and Matcha,

hearing Lionel Richie describe his natural schedule and recognizing that

it's just like mine,

thinking idly of Pete Yorn's story songs,

U2 at maximum volume in the car—the balance of a fearless, real rockstar (and the last of the truly gargantuan ones),

remembering Greg Gilbert in the mist and how he was a living rune,

then and always,

loud riff-tangles on my Explorer,

Brittania under a blanket,

and smiling like Clytemnestra who got the cream.

Plongée

There you go in your Galilee gliders,
deaf as Harpo without his horn,
running your tomography scans on helpless house sparrows,
wrecking the charabanc on the 14th-century wall of your own Lippton Village.
That beat you hear is just me wishing you were Jack.

A dancer on *Shindig* would also be my dream
the golden confidence into the elsewhere of evening.
Sure I was meant to be on Boldini's team…

One grandmother kicked the windshield out.
I think of this and how Elvis had a stammer as I am passing the lodge
where the party willfully left my beauty behind.
From my vintage hips slinks Slash on a spade,
rock tumbler rheostat and stave,
syncope and sugar kink in waves,
payless work and workless pay.

I skate along in your volcano climates aback a nifty little nostalgia,
both Hollywild and Hollyweird.
Humming Centennial songs, I am Shan Van Vocht,
rolling up the sidewalks,
dancing like dinoflagellates
—kinematic—
holding your hiccups in my hands.

Just when you think you've laid your finger on every pawn of the past,
look for a piece of the forest that doesn't fit.
You were pretty as a poster….and I was your best bit.

Soft Costs

Just a claymore knocking at your devil's door,
at my own throat,
clean contest no more.
—powder burns and the portents of Isidora.

All the wendigo ways he still chases me,
Valentina in her Enzo shoes,
half burnt out signs and street name clues,
coffee shops in movies and Italian restaurant blues,
you throttle down when I need your engine the most.

Spent our last Sunday raking your fork-tongued flattery into a pyre and setting it alight.
I don't want anyone thinking you sail under my colors anymore.
I'll take the man who cares whether his hat has European acquaintanceships
with or without him.

The Elgin marble of your excuses
—-so cold it hurts my teeth.
Plant your questions in a hedgerow for someone else to squeeze juice from
as I have no more answers to fold and refold for you.

What's better than indelicate energy in a man?
If he hasn't obviously lingered in Paris overlong, whatever could be the point?
No matter what the state of your baked lies,
I'll be ten times the man you are.

I'd like to set the house on fire just to see you run out in pajamas,
swallowing ampules of your own denatured antitoxins,
and me—
sat on your lawn fashioning castles with file-paper moats out of cigarette boxes,
—lavender and santolina overpowering the smoke.
All just to return you to your hornbeam garden room,
before dawn and your creature awoke.

Constituent Colors: Ode to a Locust-Born Butterfly
 (for Dolly Parton)

A girl, a crown, a garden.
There was stitchwort and celandine and you,
with your heavendrift hair, your A-line and ace card
tucked like torch lilies in the ditch,
not quite out of view.

You always got it and, like all truly cool people, never had to advertise that you did.
You quietly got the fact that it's hard to find pink daffodils,
and rich folks who are not confined by comfort.
You got the shoeless glory of sharecropper love stories
and guitars from Montgomery Ward.

This is why your voice enhances the kinship I always feel for the furniture
dumped on the side of the highway;
I could hear that you could still see the life it used to live,
that you could hear it singing "The Ghost of Tom Joad" just like I did.
Like rootbeer and black denim, you always make me feel retrieved.

There is still nothing like watching you
make fizzy pop out of all the flash-suppressing Boss Hoggs still out
to dim down the dreaming on the diamond dames.
You were and remain the raspberry brandy in the war cupboard.
Your albums are a fit house for all daisy-gun outlaws.
Your attitude is the only bed meet for a rhinestone rebel.
Your gold drizzle grin? An apt cloak for any aspiring blush-bandit.
I don't know if you ever yet knew: it was only Jolene who needed to worry about *you*.

Yours has always been the open church
where it didn't matter if someone had a whiskey sunburn or drawing room skills.
Atheist angels poured into peach bellbottoms,
barefoot violinists trailing tassels,
and mercurial rapscallions mangling up their turquoise tulle
could all bring their votive offerings and bog bodies to you.
Your tuneful table in the field
showed them the difference between gems and gimcrackery,
and what one life could be when it has 9-to-5 shake appeal.
Even the halo-wearing hobos who hate the spoken sound of their own names
could leave one of your shows with easier longings.
There shouldn't even be Sundays without my Mamaw and you.
—She was also from a tiny town in Tennessee and got married in Ringgold too.

Out of your oracular tradition came the only southern rhetra worth memorizing,
and the one that will echo how character is always action anonymous
when the city goes to seed.
You made people know that the heart of a woman is a portable atelier
where she dresses to suit *herself*,
never the line of men that will always be waiting outside with their lapidary looks.
If Johnny Suede don't get it, he ain't worth your electric dandelions,
your every song seemed to say.
—And this was all back when 'country' wasn't a courtesy title
and there were set measures on how far curved hips could sway.

When we began seeking our own new oceans,
all of us other chancers and chrononauts
clad in suits that could constitute crystallography classes
passed through your centrigiggle force
to learn what you already knew: life smarts harder for smart chicks.
—Especially when they sparkle through amplifiers.

They would call us
rudderless,
garrulous,
whore dust
if it hadn't been for you putting a hard candy hitch in their getalong
with your gillyflower getups,
doing Appalachian flamenco like an aubergine sunset
scattershot with mudlarks and rose farthings.
—If you hadn't jukeboxed 'em with such buttercup intensity,
all Smoky Mountain supersunshine, sung over a vibraphone melody.

Thank the stars (sky and Walk of Fame) you didn't write our path in pencil
or disappearing ink.
Your magnolia marker and many-colored coat is on all my spilt promises,
my starlit passages, and the warrior innocence of how I think.

Little Australantan me
in my sundress scramble.
The ear of my spirit caught your butterfly bouquet
all the way back in my Lawrence Welk days.
Sitting by your applewood fire, I learned my origins from your sacred steel.
You taught me to walk like a thunderbird
with that way you're always talking glittersweet bubbles
and bearing baskets of Memphis sugar as you sew parachutes for miracle stories.
You plug in the moon when you walk in my room late at night.

Sprunny

I can't believe the people I used to believe,
how ardently I searched for heartbeats beneath the snow,
wrens pecking on drums,
it's just another way to talk about weather—
—what you call affection? only palms crossed with silver.
Bezique and banana marbles
and orchard maps Smyth-sewn in a shiretown limned by marzipan moors.

For boys I really love, I become a drag king,
trying on their stance and the coat of their courage,
making plumes of their passions,
slipstreaming their satyr and making Jazz Age depravity out of their every breath.

This one I've loved for so many eddying evenings.
He had the good sense to save me for last
—and for that we never run out of firsts.
He's only just tame enough to touch;
still, you reach out your hand to August horseflesh
quivering as to a fly.
He won't swat you with his tail if you walk up right.
He is ever the earthworm writhing on the sidewalk in the afternoon light.

The Pegasus Sanctions

What most call 'politesse' is merely a bit in the mouth,
tamping the truth on one's tongue to digestible Belfast confetti.
Well, I never cared for small pieces of anything and will not be one of yours.
Give me the full dining table or let's call it done.

When even the broken pieces of your heart continue to love the one that broke them,
it is wise to realize that once they re-weld themselves together
—and if that person has not yet returned to reclaim them—
they will heal in a way that shuts that person irrevocably out.

The only map out of the ice plains is scrawled on the underside of a hat
that you traded for kindling a day before.
Icicles standing in for stained glass bouquets.
Drimwicks don't work on men made of dark days,
and there is no dictaphone in the realm that can capture your abature.

It's all a fine fettle if you fancy death by feral fetlock.
All the expansive reveries in the world can't stand you in good stead
when the heart you came in with has effortlessly split his head.
There isn't a big enough barrel of Benzocaine;
nor is there a subwoofer bleating out pink champagne.

Nectar is a fickle and fairweather feat.
Its production in flowers all depends on the creature the flower evolved to meet.
There is night-time nectar for needle-nosed bats,
and evening primrose is able to detect specific sound frequencies of bee pollinators and that
—producing "three-minute nectar" as though it were all one big bare license.

They are consecrated rattlesnakes that you wind about my neck,
rifling through my affections like an M1 Garand.
I cut my ear on your sharpened spur as I gamely brushed my cheek to your heel,
and I called the stream of blood that came just another part of the deal.
I'd bring you paper roses cut from my favorite books but
you would only use them to light your cigarettes.
No doubt I would have sat there shotgunning the plumes
—like I did your every second-hand compliment.

Your vagrant's rent is seriously in arrears.
Libations make Lyme Regis landlords of lionesses, I fear.
I had blue dots tattooed across my nose and chin—channeling Apache healers.

I wore a fluffy bomber that said "Cherry" across the back.
You took it quite literally—and put me to the rack.

This was all before we were fleeced of my cherries by your native lack
—of sweetness.
Sacred pollen plaited up with what passes for passion in your pathetic posse
—the equivalent of Tweety bird in jelly sandals, tedding hay.

Gentian and lovage (*must* it call itself that?)
tickles your eye like yellow.
Like ollieing Eel Pie Island on a Liquid Death skateboard
—it would take Tony Hawk's blood to save us.

There are places where purple peppermints are still the thing.
In these and other secret spaces, they still call her that whispered word:
"*king*."

Open Fetch

If you've got a talent for divining water, you should use it
even if they call you Hound of Deep behind your back for it.
Morality is a pretty one-dimensional system that people agree to live by.
I am always seeking the radical space.
My head is a theater of wishes;
a greater density of dreams marks my face.

Cocking my inner ear differently appears as trad climbing to the tiny fly.
I am running against the fright-ticking clock of my parents' natural life.
They've seen the loropetalum stalks, snow-broken;
they need to see the Black Shiraz I've despoiled through split-rail barricades.

One never has to mean an opening bid, after all.
I snap my fingers and turn them into a pair of sea-shod chariot ponies.
This way they will be sweet-hitched to the front of my starfish epidemic for all their days.

Back when my freedom was wet paint
and we were all playing drunken polo on donkeys,
spilling bottles of champagne in bathtubs full of nine people,
I was of the red ocher religion
and wore a necklace of four pigeon heads.
I wanted to be like Budgie—kestrels and goshawks, taiko and gamelan.
I deserved a Croix de Guerre for what I'd already been:

An arch privateer to out-of-date boys.

Best Legs in the Baptist Church

this generation longs so to be famous
not knowing
celebrity loses a certain something under the flash of your own camera
not seeing
I only steal because I cannot appreciate anything until it is my own

Do you twig?

you can have the best legs in the whole Baptist church
you can watch them try not to sigh and lurch
in your direction

it's God's will they should look away
something more primal makes their eyes go gray

Chaperone Shoes

Daughters of bonafide rockstars are forever looking for a Country Gentleman,
one cast in the sun-mold of George Harrison would especially do.
Instead you'll get a bluff Aries—or even two.
Worse, you might inherit an Appalachian love.
Some people find adoration so much easier to give where it isn't owed.
Some godly reminders most certainly do not originate from any Olympian place above.

Don't do it—it's a trap.
You are governed by such different golden proportions than they.
Your nights with them won't know this. Neither will their days.
Trust me: the local yokels will only want to siphon the "borrowed" fuel of your own potential.
All the while, they will quietly despise you for feeding them,
spitting sand into the engine every time you turn your back.
A toad on a paving stone never had such a view of himself.
Don't let frivolity fox your features—because it *will*.
You're too young to know, but you'll change your mind
once you're too old to go.
You've no idea how young you have to be before your ideas are your own
and no longer the homesteaded property of your advanced age.

Both kinds of hothouse impostors will know nothing of where wildflowers preside.
They will refuse to be blue-gold. They will bow like tired-trodden floor boards.
Neither will have the courage to bite through your skin,
too shaky from void of character to get that close to anything but gin.
Hubris-hobbled to their lecterns of failure,
they'll always run for pedestrian mother-cover,
straight from the cut-em-out clinic—yet again.
They'll laugh at a distance
trying to sport-poison you from afar with their blown venom
—suburban snobhearted junkie-Houyhnhnms.

Think of dames like Amanda De Cadenet if it is babies you inexplicably want:
twins by none other than Nick Valensi and a Duran Duran daughter
off our own John Taylor.
Now, *that's* how you stop rearranging the cushions of Gaia-life and get on with it.
In all other instances, when the drums of marriage are sounding,
clasp mane on the nearest fleet horse and *flee*.

If you're at all smart, you will save your saving for yourself.
The colours *will* make their best and final show

and you would do well to remember how
you thought a hundred bucks was a whole lotta love-money
not such a long time ago.

Hail Mary Pass
    (one last-sung song for a lost Lorelai)

You've curled up and died in his condensed swirls like a licked leopard slug,
eight days of solid silence
and then a shuddering shrug.
I orchestrate my chance encounters with your keeled tales,
summoning the dapple grays and dancing past the doubters—
I unfurl our sails—against all odds.
Especially yours.

I still like anything in a lemon print;
I still twirl in the Tuileries and know what Borogoves meant.

Driving a Teardrop Talbot-Lago,
with all your colors sick-fading
but still matching the notes of any mixolydian scale,
You relinquish all possible Amapianos
—all your Cherokee freedoms now fully embargoed.

This is where you laugh your last
This is what you call 'handfast.'

Wings of Wax on the Dais

You never want to stop the day before it's done.
So you walk in the late light
fat-struggling your way to the top of the mile-high mountain
that keeps your house so forever shaded.

From the summit you drip sweat from your ear lobes
and look out across the top of another mountain,
the same one on the other side of which live the wolves and Gibbons and fennecs
you visited with your Mom earlier today.

Only a few hours ago
in this same daylight.

You feel like you can see Gideon, the alpha wolf, and can still hear sloths crunching carrots
you handed them from amazed hands.
An airplane streaking across the sky is wearing the sounds of all the places you're not.

Can Gideon hear it?

Your destiny will always be built on the days you don't feel like it.

June Plum

I've been around to all my friends;
I've been let out and stayed shut in.
I've walked at midnight and slept at noon,
Through stalactite light,
and it is still June.

I've written three sonnets and one half-song,
I sang them right but played them wrong.
I'm circling again in the timeless bright,
and it is only ever still June.

the little now is a riot of nuance
a tiny square of scone
slow traffic
Saturday sunset music
chariots of glass
posies and patches

you wanted me in turnkey condition so
you posed me in every position,
and all of this while it was only still June.

I soar through the mosaic flowers;
I talk to Cypriot doves for hours,
summer is the last childhood honeymoon.
I'm 32 now—
and it is soon once again to be June.

Atomic Heels

I caged up all your jailbirds and made them sing my name,
just like your junkie son did behind your back the night the stars blew out.
But oh how I worship your rotten little heart,
your kiss in the psychedelic flower bed—glowing on my lips for nights on end,
the knotted roots where our fingers wed.

She wore her most atomic heels—colored torches close the deal…

It was our best flamingo sunset that did them in for good,
just for time and its corollary.
But no, I don't hate your honey hands.
Your dure bounty lives in uneven complexions.

I will come to you, naked but for my wings,
No one ever yet slept on the floor because of me.
But when you hate the way it sounds to say your own name,
summer in February and the after-show letdown—the boy with the absinthe egg,
and me in Cleopatra's gown.

She snapped her most atomic heels—witching sticks of rose and teal…

Cold Air Pictures

Standing on sullied stardust, the nomenclature of the clouds
was sacred geometry and Jean Cocteau
and fluoro-fusion porno to me.
I quickly set about alphabetizing a library of sounds for the aural-ambrette illiterate.

I wanted (and still want) to look like I once nonchalantly dated Baltazhar Getty.
I can see him coming when I don't look,
making my colors fast—perpetrator as recreation.
I was chasing the Draupner Wave but I found only various forms of Datura along my way,
always beckoning in the guise of a masculinized devanagari script,
or a neon dated dayrunner.

Waving a trumpet and a candy cane, I kept fervently praying
I could sing my steps around all the organophosphate rain bubbling up from the ground
and threatening to eat the edges off my eager Lizard King costume.
There was a heart-cherry there in the sedge hassocks,
flailing in the quicksand of his own bile.
From him I learned the Haviland patterns in laceration
and that people who have never felt unbridled joy also cannot imagine it.

Your mid-level responses are mindfucks.
Your painted-on F-holes are gettin' mossy.
Meanwhile, I'm dreamily scratching 'Eire' in my forearm in cursive blood
and drawing a lemon bicycle with key-lime wheels,
all while I live like a leaf on a string of silken spiderweb
that you yo-yo bounce over mulch you haven't paid for yet
—and don't know when you'll have the money to.

There was never a cavalcade me for you to kick around
—and I can still feel you seething over that.
Even baby me was freer than you will ever be. (The real bee in your cap)
She could be found playing imaginatively with the cardboard applicators of vintage tampons,
as those were as alien to her as any of your crepitating cuneiforms, and every bit as useless.
Driving back from the casino in the dark with pistachio muffin crumbs carefully balanced
in my lap because I am too nostalgic to stop and toss them out of the car door, I remember
her.
I *bless* her.
She, like me, was not to be closed in by your children and your crepiness.
Black-purple lipstick, gold disco capes, white Grecian ancestress dresses
—poor torche-cul….

you'll *never* catch us.

I Atalanta-run right back to the now.
No more for me your razorwire Maypole or the skyless thatch of your eyeless fire fight.
Your sheep-stench surfactants and defeated exodus will prop up your gerontocracy
—until they don't—but I won't.
I am wearing the wounds of another world,
knowing the last of the iron-slain Fenrirs by all their first names,
deep-sworn and bone-bound to the gentle pillage of a much older chieftain
—and his are cunning spells, speaking of reaping spirits.
My king keeps a piano in his hedge, brushing his swiveled ear only on the white keys as he whisks by, his carrion-clipped hair a riot of rose madder and burnt gold.

On the far red hill, I can still see them.
Your northern ponies stand, hunched in a bunch, backs turned,
sweltering against my never-setting sun.
The horses that wouldn't drink. Closer to death than they will ever think.
You, like they, will never understand anything that could have saved your life,
much less that it was all down to my hooves and the Sinead-legs they were attached to.
It wasn't even the fleet feet of the money, something else you'll never get.
It was that part about how I will not take my purple-jeweled cuff off until the last thing at
night because I wore it all day on my adventures with my precious mother
when she was proudly showing me her blue leopard shirt and laughing as she spilt my water.
The bracelet has all that (and all her) all in it.
Like me.
Like color vision, all of this was all only ever about opponency.

Moon Madlings

Well done, us!
No one ever saw us tumble out of the grandfather clock, one after the other
like so many Bacha Posh acrobats,
seconds ahead of being conspicuously late to dinner yet again.
We were always conspiratorially chased by a brace of over-friendly rooks,
our palms coated in negligible nectarine, drowned scone smidgens and squid giggles
falling freely from our peacoat pockets in a techno-pastoral candy-crumb trail like no other.

Pendulum pirates, we were!
Wee nixies of the wry-necked variety,
we danced on the escritoire with our escargot governess and
spent our afternoons playing imperial concertina to the
talking apple trees,
blissfully adrift in a world balanced atop a banquet table of overturned canoes
(in which we set up hermitage)
and purple velvet top hats
from which we drew no end of magician rabbits, sextets, and spiralized marbles.

Between banana leaves, in balloon sleeves and loudly checked trousers,
we took in the beatitudes and other rare wisdoms shared with us
by a paradise of best-friend donkeys.
In our butcher's boy bonnets we brayed right in tune with them, boxing the boxwood
hedgerows for their verdant impertinence,
blowing dizzy pinwheels round and round the cricket carousels
while chips of beggar granite that were really square-cut emeralds
emptied from our willow-woven pouches.
All appeared a graceful gambol of divine disgrace. All forgot to forget time.

No one ever had to invent Christmas for us!
Not for us any stale Savile Row suspenders or stealsome Steerforth storm-shanties.
Smacks of jellyfish formed our carpets and Sedgemoor geese (our sentinels and soldiers)
flew in full fleabitten regalia.
Up and up the skinna-ma-rink spiral staircase where it was forever Saturday we skipped,
chimera-cat kites in tow, kerchiefs dutifully askew around eager foreheads,
socks slinking at separate speeds like a rigged race of mismatched inchworms
down coltish legs already bramble-run to blue-black bruises.
Primed to picnic on gingerbread and currant trifle in our public library of gorse and heather,
we made a sport of counting the gold buttons worn by our mouse footmen
even as we pulled faces in their aurelian reflections.

Off we then pirouetted across the Victorian Goonie planks,
their strigose squeaks a Spirograph symphony we deliberately played
as well or better as ever did Wolfgang his zebra keys,
wicking cockles and cake from our crumpled quartos of Brontës even as we spun.

They say half of nothing is nothing;
to you and me, it was two of everything,
and because of this we more than thrice-doubled the anythings
we still know we could be.
Well done, us.

Acknowledgments

Not a spot of this collection's ink would have ever existed outside of my unstructured imagination without a slew of supernatural supporters and sidekicks I have been unspeakably fortunate to have in my life since its artistic inception.

First and foremost: my parents. Kay Montgomery, Danny Miller, Kerry Montgomery, and Karen Miller, for working so hard to ensure that I had the best of things in this life, both emotional and material, and most importantly: for showing me which of those was the only one that carried weight. Mom, thank you for the wild legions of leopard-print laughter. Dad, thank you for the eternal education of the music. Kerry and Karen, thank you for loving me as though it was your biological imperative. Thank all of you for every single one of the opportunities your love selflessly bought me. My sister, Lindsey Miller–my "favorite" (and only) sibling–for suspecting and vocalizing long before I did the idea that I was meant to be a professional writer, and for expressing nothing but admiration for my pursuit of the words that you alone already knew were mine.

My treasured friends: Shawn Carter for proving day in and day out what tangible and everlasting loyalty looks like and that all of the most golden wizards are dark ones. Devin Downs for our mind-reading magic and those many things only *you* understand about me. Matt Weickert for always reminding me what to run *toward* and for your everlasting depth of listening. Liridon Hajrizi for being the physical embodiment of fable-level friendship at all times, as well as the first and last guest at every party. Hector and Christy Amador for always believing in what I do enough to want to photograph it in high definition technicolor. Mitchell Williford for never letting me lose faith in what true Disney princes can be by being the best one of them all, and for actively protecting me from the worst of everything since forever. Ashlee Newsome Williford for helping me continue to know that wild-woman duchesses do indeed collide with and increase the overall worth of such princes in this life and far beyond. Jonnie and Linda Botts, for a caliber of continuous, all-encompassing support and universal love that should be taught as an emotional foundation in every school. Jessica Kavanaugh for physically dragging my dreams back from the dead with her bare hands and making me open every door and window in the soul of my life in her efforts to remind me I am a Sun Child. Stacey Heale for opening the door to so many of my most aerial wishes, both ethereal and corporeal, and doing it like you had been expecting me. Nicola Musgrove for casting so many inimitable healing spells over one of the hardest times of my life and every day since. Timmy Musgrove for being my real-deal Dickon Sowerby from *The Secret Garden* that I was always looking for my whole life and will forever require. Rhys Griffiths for saving me time and again with the greatest puns on the planet and the most mystical Welsh wisdom imaginable. Richard Fitz-Thomas for making me laugh harder than anybody can and being my eternal hero-brother that I would trust with my life. And Marilynn Richtarik for giving me my true introduction to Irish scholarship and being the unassailably high benchmark by which I will always measure myself both personally and professionally. Also: Matt Bolch, LaCheyna Sparrow, Neva Corbin, Betty Cali, Dottie Taylor, Tommy Houseman, Michele Berryman, Sam Dunaway, Cathie Kobsa Fennell, John and Nancy Crews, Sue Armitage, James Chapman, Paul and Kathryn Garthwaite, Jason Smith, Dana and Camille Burkett, Wesley and Charlotte Carr, Sophie B. Hawkins, Ethan Ballinger, Matt Pollock, Joe Bleakley, Seth Hendershot, Jessica Hayes, Anthony J. Resta, and Kathleen Fowlds—all of the above for so many life-saving reasons that it would take lifetimes of full-length books to even scratch the shallowest surface of. You all know why and how I will always adore you, and I wholeheartedly thank each one of you in your irreplaceable ways for keeping the volume turned up to a respectable Spinal Tap "11" on my glitter at all times, but especially during those times when others were actively trying to turn those sparkles down for reasons of their own killing-comfort. Thank you for not allowing it. In that refusal, thank you for allowing space for *me*.

Gargantuan gratitude goes to the psychobilly duo of all time that is Hot Rod Walt and his lady-queen Sharlene Richards for their expertise in the creation of the incendiary cover image for this book, as well as for years of fun, fiery inspiration of all sorts. Likewise, all the scintillating appreciation in the fairy world to Jana Brandelik for taking my formal author's photos and also for shooting the first pictures of my recognized artistic life some time ago in a school bus graveyard only we could have found.

My living rock heroes: Paul Hewson, Cyndi Lauper, Mark Knopfler, Colin Hay, Thom Yorke, Roger Manning, Pete Yorn, and Jack White III. For demonstrating what singular greatness means with your every breath and being the reason I first knew what I am. And the heavyweight champion of them all in the galvanizing starlight category for me: Craig Robert Nicholls. For making me see myself fully for the first time ever and at a juncture in my life when I had no other human means through which to learn what it *really* meant to be a *real* rogue wave, as well as for demonstrating to me what unflappable courage and artistic conviction look like in the flesh, on the biggest stages of the world no less. Had there been no you, Wallaby King, there surely never would have been an unburied, cut-free me, nor any of my life's favorite days, against which the tribulations of spirit captured in this book evaporate like whispered words on the wind.

My Otherside wonders: I salute the twin lodestars of my faithful fairytale-departed: Kurt Cobain, for modeling to me how it looked to do right things the right way against all odds, and Greg Gilbert, for being the brightest human star-angel on any plane of existence ever, and one who is only ever as far as my next blink from my creative inspiration. Most vital in this over-the-rainbow category is my Mamaw, Helen Louise Miller, the most formative influence my life has ever or will ever see. If I am ever sweet or patient in the slightest, it is only because of Mamaw.

The word-women who lit the way for me: I have spent the entirety of my life actively dreaming of being anything at all like Emily Brontë, Elizabeth Bowen, Jane Austen, Sylvia Plath, Virginia Woolf, A.S. Byatt, Iris Murdoch, and Donna Tartt. Each one of them sits astride the shoulder of any interesting thing I have ever managed to wrangle out of the sky and onto the paper. I owe them much more than my perseverance and pages; I am indebted to them for the particular bent of most of my literary thoughts. Thank you, ladies, for writing for your life so that I would know I could and should do the same.

I likewise give solemn recognition to the unnameable, serpentine demons of my experience, those soul-sick suppressors who labored their Luciferian longest to lacerate my life and whose unwarranted venom, injected into me for the purpose of killing off what was best in my bloodstream, failed spectacularly (as demons must where wings abound). In such attempted murder, you only gave me the warrior-wounds through which these pixie-passions poured, and thus the power to become permanent poison to your kind forevermore–with and without my piranha-pen in tow. May your poison remain ever as ineluctable as your fame.

Lastly, all the sparkly ink of my heart to the editors and publishers who have put me in proper print over the years. I still stand amazed at your belief in me, a feeling I know will never diminish, and my reverence for you is matched only by my gratitude.

Postscript Magazine—"Spent Force"
Better Than Starbucks—"Wavelet Well Met"
Nauseated Drive—"MX-76," "Last Lighthouses," and "It Glows Under The Half-Smirk"
Sledgehammer Lit—"Gannets"
FERAL: A Journal of Poetry and Art—"Printed With Ibex"
Small Leaf Press—"My Time and Other Gate-Kept Institutions"
Tofu Ink Arts Press—"Recrucify, Then Rewind" and "Last Halloween in Hawaii"
Streetlights Magazine—"MX-76"
Ink, Sweat, and Tears—"High July"
The Pangolin Review—"High July"
Cerasus Magazine—"Moon Madlings," "Hail Mary Pass," "Tattered Empress," "Imbuvable Indigo," and "Dybbuk of my Daymares"
Green Ink Poetry—"Manannan mac Lir"
The Purpled Nail—"Moon Madlings"
Cape Magazine—"Multum In Parvo" and "Double Termination Points"
Ghost City Press—"Last Halloween in Hawaii"
ChillFltr—"Moon Madlings"
Tigershark Magazine—"Dybbuk of my Daymares"
The Opiate—"Marmaduchess" and "Best Legs in the Baptist Church"
Wayward Literature—"Mint Metallic"
Cream Scene Carnival—"Entrechats Wearing Radio Collars"
The Avenue—"Sauterelle"

Dana Miller is a wicked wordsmith, giggling provocateuse, and mega-melomaniac from Atlanta, Georgia. Her poetic syllables like to trundle in the wilds—usually in search of a Pooh-like smackerel or two. On their way, they have found themselves featured in *Postscript Magazine, Better Than Starbucks, Fairy Piece, FERAL: A Journal of Poetry and Art, Sledgehammer Lit, ChillFiltr Review, Small Leaf Press, Tofu Ink Press,* and *Nauseated Drive*. Her journalistic works have found their faces in places like *L.A. Weekly, OK Magazine, Grazia, Maxim, Women's World,* and *International Business Times*. When not wielding a lethal pen, Dana adores surf culture, Australian grunge rockers, muscle cars, Epiphone guitars, glitter, Doc Martens, and medieval-looking draft horses with feathered feet. Oxford, England is her spirit-home and Radiohead is holding the last shard of her girlhood heart. Dana has completed all coursework for a Doctorate in Modernist Literature and is making headway through her dissertation on Anglo-Irish women writers with her research focusing primarily on ideas of female ferality in Modernist Hibernian writers. With no biological understanding of small ambitions, she keeps a cauldron of creative writing projects ever-bubbling toward long-form, large-scale publishing goals. When those frequently untended cauldrons bubble over all at once and stain the floor with sparkles, she then claims those scintillating flecks on the floor are intentional art too. If Dana is not at home writing in unicorn pajamas with a Cadbury Fruit & Nut close at hand, she is likely down the rock-n-roll highway with an untamed Oz band or merrily lost in the forest somewhere near her mountain cottage. *Never Née Fey* is her first full-length book of poetry.

www.ingramcontent.com/pod-product-compliance
Lightning Source LLC
Chambersburg PA
CBHW020339170426
43200CB00006B/435